THE COMMON ROCKS AND MINERALS OF MISSOURI

W. D. KELLER

UNIVERSITY OF MISSOURI PRESS • COLUMBIA

University of Missouri Press, Columbia, Missouri 65201
ISBN 0-8262-0585-2
Library of Congress Card Number 67-66173
Printed and bound in the United States of America
All rights reserved
First Edition 1945
Revised Editions 1948, 1961
Reprinted 1971, 1973, 1978, 1986, 1989, 1992, 2004

TABLE OF CONTENTS

INTRODUCTION

Missourians are interested in the rocks and minerals which they find on their farms, in excavations, and while on their vacation trips. Some of the specimens are unusual in shape or appearance, some are crystalline and beautiful, some may be ores of economic importance, but many simply arouse the curiosity of the finder.

Many of these specimens are received each year at the University at Columbia, and each is usually accompanied by a request for information on the correct name for the specimen, its composition, its commercial value, and the manner of its formation.

Frequently the requests include questions of a broader geological nature, or seek the recommendation of a general, easily-read book written on rocks and minerals which may be purchased at a book store or consulted at a library. Moreover, many persons ask how they may determine for themselves the geological specimens which they have collected.

This little booklet has been prepared with the intention of answering the questions most commonly asked by citizens of the state about Missouri rocks and minerals.

Descriptions and photographs of Missouri rock and mineral occurrences are provided, and essential facts about the geological conditions of their formation are simply told. A determinative key is supplied in order that the reader may identify and name most of the common specimens which he collects within the state (and elsewhere, also). No special determinative equipment will be suggested, and only non-technical language will be employed because the chief objective here is to furnish a useful, understandable geological account of the *common* Missouri rocks and minerals to the average person without geological training. In fact, for the purposes of identification no differentiation is made between mineral and rock, although the professional geologist does separate them in definition. For our purpose, a rock is an aggregate of mineral particles, but a mineral is a substance (without life) having more definite and constant properties than a rock. For those interested further, more technical and more nearly correct definitions, with explanations, are given at the back, on page 74.

The rarer minerals and those requiring special equipment for determination may be sent to the Department of Geology of the University of Missouri at Columbia for identification free of charge.*

Names used locally, and sometimes incorrectly from a strictly technical sense, for rocks and minerals will follow the generally accepted names, and·both will be duplicated in the index at the back of the pamphlet to facilitate finding either one.

DETERMINATIVE KEY

A rock or mineral specimen which is unfamiliar to the collector may be identified by using the information in this booklet in either of two ways: (1) the reader may turn through the pages and compare his specimen with the photographs of others named there and read their descriptions until he finds a match for his specimen; or (2), the better way, he may classify his specimen first by the use of the determinative key which follows and be directed thereby to the pages in the book for confirmation of the name by the photographs, description, and discussion of the substance. The writer recommends the second method and has prepared this booklet on the assumption that the determinative key will be used.

The simplest and probably the best means of separating specimens of different rocks and minerals is on the basis of hardness, which means *resistance to scratching*. Crushing strength is different from hardness; therefore, in testing for hardness, do not attempt to pulverize. Merely determine if the specimen can be scratched with the substance indicated.

Determination of the mark or "streak" of a mineral when rubbed on a hard white rock or unglazed porcelain is demonstrated in the photograph on page 56.

A. Specimens that can be scratched readily with the THUMB NAIL.

    1. Become muddy when rubbed with a wet finger.

*This service is also offered by the Department of Geology, Missouri School of Mines and Metallurgy, Rolla, Missouri, and by the State Geologist, Rolla, Missouri.

11. Looks like rosin, or may be ruby-colored or blåck, but has a high resinous luster on freshly broken surface.
    SPHALERITE 60
12. Glassy luster; water-white, milky, honey-colored, pink, gray; may occur in six-sided crystals, sometimes pyramid-shaped; always breaks with flat glistening faces; always reacts in the lump with cold dilute muriatic (hydrochloric) acid.
    CALCITE 16
13. Like calcite above but may have a pink, pearly luster and curved crystal faces; reacts with cold dilute acid when powdered but not readily in lump form.
    DOLOMITE 18
14. Opaque white, glassy or bluish, very heavy, lustrous on freshly broken surface; does not react with acid.
    BARITE 61
15. Flaky, micaceous like "isinglass".
    MICA 44

C. Specimens TOO HARD to be scratched readily on a fresh surface with a pocket knife or iron nail; weathered specimens may be slightly scratched.
    1. Very fine-grained throughout, compact; occurs in nodules, pebbles; breaks with a slick, curved, oyster-shell-like (conchoidal) fracture.
       CHERT, if white, gray or stained yellow or red 34
       FLINT, if black 34
       AGATE, if banded 37
       PETRIFIED WOOD, if it shows the grain or bark of wood 37
    2. Granular like sandstone but extremely hard and breaks through the grains as readily as around them.
       QUARTZITE 41
       QUARTZITIC SANDSTONE 30
    3. Fine-grained, dark green to dark gray to greenish black; occurs in boulders north of Missouri River and in the granite and porphyry country or southeastern Missouri.
       BASALT 46
    4. Very fine-grained, compact, pink, red, brown, gray; usually "freckled" or sprinkled with grains about $\frac{1}{16}$ inch in diameter.
       PORPHYRY 45
       RHYOLITE 45
       RHYOLITE PORPHYRY 45
    5. Coarse-grained (BB-shot size to considerably larger), glassy luster where freshly broken; pink, red, grey.
       GRANITE 38
       GNEISS, like granite but *banded*; occurs in boulders north of the Missouri River 38

ROCK AND MINERAL DESCRIPTIONS
Limestone and Dolomite

Limestone is a bedded or layered rock found abundantly in Missouri in bluffs, creek beds, hill sides, and is known to underlie the soil in most of the south half of the state. It occurs in thin slabs, thick layers, and in massive beds which may make a small cliff in themselves. Limestone is soft enough to be scratched with steel. It is commonly white to grayish, but may be stained tan, yellowish, or reddish by iron oxide, or darkened through shades of gray to black by the presence of very finely-divided, black carbonaceous matter. It may be microscopically fine-grained (and then it can be used in lithographic printing in the reproduction of very fine images), or its grains may vary in size up to one-half inch in cross section.

Limestone (dolomite) bluff near Jefferson City.

It is determined as limestone with certainty by wetting with dilute cold acid; then it "bubbles" or effervesces, and eventually dissolves entirely. Ordinary or regular limestone contains the mineral calcite, but the magnesian variety of limestone, dolomite, contains the mineral dolomite, which does not effervesce freely in lump size in dilute acid, but which does effervesce when *powdered* or when treated with hot acid or concentrated acid. The preferred acid to use is muriatic (hydrochloric, the "not-cut" soldering acid) diluted one part of acid to one part of water. Caution! This acid mixture should be stored in a glass or porcelain container away from children or animals! Acid strong enough to dissolve rock will ruin clothes, destroy flesh, and is poisonous! Dilute sulphuric (storage battery) acid will also give the effervescence test, and the acid of very strong vinegar will react with limestone slowly.   In making the test it should be recognized that the limestone which acts as a cement in sandstone, or limestone impurities in shale will also effervesce, but those minor parts of the rock will dissolve and leave the residues of sandstone or shale, which are insoluble.

A coarse-grained limestone effervescing in dilute muriatic acid.   (This photograph and other close-up views taken by J. F. Barham and Allen Barnes, University photographers.)

Solid dolomite does *not* effervesce in dilute acid. Note the white rock powder scrapings adjacent.

Dolomite powder does effervesce in dilute muriatic acid.   Not all dolomite is this fine in grain.

Some limestones are chemical deposits but many are consolidated accumulations of fossil shells and shell fragments—organic limestone. For example, a widespread limestone, the so-called Burlington limestone, extending across central Missouri, contains many crinoid stem fragments and plates, attesting to the abundance of crinoids living in the sea at the time this limestone was laid down. Crinoids are sea animals which, because of their branching structure and superficial resemblance to plants, have been nicknamed "sea lilies." Except for calcareous cave and spring deposits, almost all limestone formations in Missouri contain a few fossils of animals which lived in the ocean, and therefore Missouri limestones are considered marine in origin. They offer evidence for the very interesting land-sea changes which this state has undergone in the geologic past.

Limestone composed almost entirely of crinoid (marine animal fossil) stem plates, from near Columbia.

Pure limestone is composed of 100% calcium carbonate (calcite mineral), whereas pure dolomite contains 54.35% calcium carbonate and 45.65% magnesium carbonate (dolomite mineral). Magnesium carbonate has slightly higher acid-neutralizing properties than calcium carbonate, weight for weight, and because analyses of limestone to be used for soil sweetening and agricultural fertilizer purposes are commonly reported in calcium carbonate equivalents, a dolomite or dolomitic limestone may be reported over 100% calcium carbonate equivalent. Unless one understands the full meaning of the report he may be bewildered by a statement of the value over 100%.

The calcium and magnesium which form limestone (or dolomitic limestone) in the ocean are carried there in solution by the streams which drain the land. Rain water percolating through the ground and rocks becomes slightly acidified with carbon dioxide (like the carbonated water in beverages) and dissolves the calcium and magnesium from primary igneous rocks like gabbro and basalt which are weathering, or from preexisting limestones which primitively were derived from igneous rocks. This calcium and magnesium in solution are responsible for the hardness of the water. In fact, the hard water in Missouri springs, wells, and streams is hard because it contains either or both calcium ("lime") and magnesium in solution.

This soluble calcium and magnesium flows on in the stream to the ocean because of its combination with the dissolved carbon dioxide. In the shallow parts of the ocean, as on the continental shelves where the water is less than 600 feet deep, the limestone is deposited in layers just like the white lime layer deposits on the bottom of the teakettle in which hard water has been boiled. Chemical processes, temperature changes, evaporation of the ocean water, and organisms are responsible for most of the limestone deposition. Extensive limestone deposition is taking place today off the coast of Florida and around the tropical islands of the southern Pacific.

The uses of limestone are numerous. It is an excellent building stone in either the rough, sawn, or dressed state. It is used for rubble stone, rip-rap, railroad ballast, crushed gravel, and aggregate in concrete. It is one of the raw materials of Portland cement. Quicklime and hydrated lime are prepared from limestone which has been heated to drive off the chemically combined carbon dioxide.

Limestone is added as a fluxing material in metallurgical processes. It is the lowest priced source of alkali in chemical industry. Pulverized limestone may be used as a filler in paints, putty, paper, or rubber; and rock wool is made by melting and blowing a limestone having a suitable chemical composition. Two formations develop a "spongy" appearance ("sponge rock" or "sponge limestone") upon weathering and are utilized abundantly in the eastern part of the state for rock gardens and for ornamental and decorative stone.

Many tons of limestone are used each year in Missouri as a soil fertilizer because it neutralizes acidity, coagulates the clay, furnishes calcium to the plants by way of the colloidal clay, and frees other chemical elements so that they become available to the plants. No doubt rocks other than limestone will be crushed and added to the soil in the future, but today our attention is focussed chiefly on limestone and dolomite.

The value of a limestone quarry for agricultural purposes depends upon availability, amount of overburden, purity of the stone, ease of crushing, and size of deposit. For instance, a stone of 90% purity, which is close at hand, will probably be more valuable than one of 98% purity which must be hauled fifteen miles. Bare hillsides or creek banks where a crusher can be set up to handle the stone without extra lifting are preferable for quarry sites. Usually the overburden is less in such an exposed face. Impurities in limestone deposits may be large chert (flint) nodules which can be hand-sorted out, sand grains, clay which settled into and onto the stone during its accumulation, and pyrite (fool's gold) or other minerals of lesser importance. Clay impurities simply act as useless extra weight which must be handled. Sand grains, however, are hard, and will abrade and wear out crushing equipment. Chert and fine-grained silica likewise are harder than steel and will wear a crusher excessively. Pure limestone (calcite or dolomite mineral) has a hardness less than that of steel and will only polish or wear the metal slightly.

Typical, intermittently-operated, farm limestone quarry near North Kansas City.

It will probably pay to give some thought to this matter of crushing when selecting a quarry site for agricultural limestone. The several beds of stone available should be tested not only for amount, but kinds of impurities. Samples sent in for testing must be *representative* of the rocks under consideration or the analytical results are meaningless. The writer does not believe this point can be over-emphasized. Time after time he has seen samples taken of geological deposits for testing which no more represented the deposits than a bantam rooster picked out of a chicken pen would represent the egg-laying or weight-production possibilities of the flock of Plymouth Rock hens.

If five layers or beds of stone are to be properly tested, then five samples must be taken, *one broken from each layer of solid rock in place.* The five layers may have the same color, or look much the same, but fine grains of sand, hardly visible without magnification, may be abundant in some layers and not in others. If circumstances do not permit having five different tests made, but allow only one sample to be run, then specimens should be taken from all five beds, their sizes being in proportion to the relative amounts expected to be quarried from each bed, and all five specimens sent to the analyst, who can crush and mix them.

A single grab sample taken from loose rock on a hillside, in expectation that it will represent the rocks inside, depends as much on luck as betting on the weather next 4th of July, a year hence. The chemist who analyzes the limestone for calcium can usually report on the kind of impurity if he will take the time to do it.

"Cotton Rock" Limestone

"Cotton rock" refers to a white to slightly gray or buff variety of limestone which has a "soft", somewhat chalky and porous appearance that is suggestive of cotton. Missouri "cotton rock" is usually dolomitic. Although the term "cotton rock" has no standing in a technical sense, its fairly wide use indicates that the name has descriptive value.

Marble

Marble, in a scientific sense, is a metamorphic rock and does not occur as such in Missouri. However, marble has been used as a name in commercial trade to refer to a crystalline, fairly pure limestone, which possesses most of the useful qualities of true marble. In that sense the "marbles" quarried near Ozora and Carthage, Missouri, are very excellent stone. No doubt some recrystallization has occurred in connection with the faulting in the Ozora region, and this may be interpreted as mild metamorphism. The Carthage "marble" is quarried from beds of limestone well developed for structural purposes. These "marbles" effervesce in acid, of course, just as described for limestone.

In this connection it is interesting to note that the polish on limestone or marble is not durable where exposed to the weather in the same sense as is the polish on granite. Because limestone and marble are softer than granite they may be cut and polished at lower cost, but because of their ease of attack by acid, water, and abrasion they soon become dull when used as an exterior stone. For interior decoration they are excellent, of course. Granite contains hard minerals which happen not to be attacked appreciably by dilute acids, and therefore it retains a polish for a long time even where exposed to the weather.

Cave Onyx and Deposits

The stalactites (rock icicles) hanging from cave ceilings, stalagmites built up from the floors, and other drip stone deposits of caves are largely calcite, the mineral of limestone. Again, this can be recognized by the limestone acid test (effervescence, see limestone). Cave onyx may be banded like agate. It is then commonly called Mexican onyx. The name travertine has also been applied to such deposits from water.

Travertine

Travertine is a general name for calcium carbonate deposits of varying size, shape, color, texture, and purity which originate largely through evaporation of spring or surface water. Its composition of calcium carbonate, calcite mineral, is easily confirmed by effervescence in acid, like limestone.

Calcite

Calcite (sometimes called "tiff" locally in south-*western* Missouri), the essential mineral in limestone, can be recognized by several definite characteristics:

1. It bubbles, "fizzes," or *effervesces* in dilute acid. See page 11.
2. It is easily scratched with a knife.
3. It breaks or cleaves into rhombohedral shapes, of which at least one flat, glistening side is visible on every individual grain in the broken surface of limestone.
4. It has a glassy luster on crystal and cleavage faces.
5. It crystallizes into six-sided crystal forms, which can be differentiated from quartz (also six-sided) by tests (1) and (2) above.

The one single test of calcite which is most diagnostic, and which appeals to most persons, is number one above, effervescence of the solid lump in dilute acid. The bubbles are filled by carbon dioxide gas which comes from, and is freed from, the calcite by the reaction of it with the acid. Calcite is calcium carbonate, $CaCO_3$.

A small calcite crystal from the Joplin region.

Many Missourians have not realized that the ordinary, every-day limestone (fine to coarse granular), which is so abundant here, is composed of a mineral—calcite which makes up the grains. The strikingly beautiful calcite crystals (displayed in museums) derived from the calcite crystal caves found in some mines in the Joplin district are accepted without question as *mineral* specimens of calcite, but the idea that all of the commonplace glistening grains in the local limestone are also mineral grains is a new thought to most persons. A pure limestone is composed entirely of calcite. Even impure limestones which contain subordinate amounts of quartz sand, chert, clay, or iron oxide are in the main also calcite. Dolomite and dolomitic limestones contain the mineral dolomite.

The mineral of ordinary marble is calcite; dolomite marble contains dolomite. The cementing material in sandstone and a common accessory mineral in shale are calcite. It is truly a wide-spread and abundant mineral. Even the lime deposit in the bottom of the tea-kettle, the water heater, boiler, or automobile cooling system is calcite, or aragonite, a twin brother to calcite.

The use of calcite in the form of limestone is treated under limestone. As for the use of large calcite crystals, they are sold as ornaments and curiosities. Visitors to the Missouri State Fair may recall the exhibit of a beautiful, reconstructed crystal cave which was lined with large calcite crystals. Calcite crystals have been shipped in car-load lots to beautify grottos, notably some in Iowa and Illinois, and are displayed in almost all prominent museums.

Water-white (clear), optical-quality calcite crystals, which command a high price, are relatively rare and have not been found in Missouri.

The optical property of calcite which accounts for its high value is its ability to separate, or refract, every single ray of light passing through it into two widely separated, easily distinguishable rays, hence doubling their number. This is called double refraction, and is shown by the double image of an object viewed through the calcite. Instruments which polarize light may contain calcite crystals. The artificial product, "Polaroid", is used for a similar purpose.

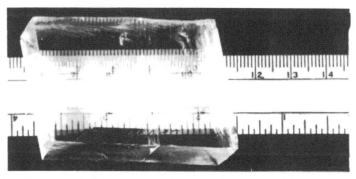

Calcite cleavage rhomb, characteristic rhombohedral shape. Note the double image due to high double refraction of calcite.

Dolomite

Dolomite mineral occurs in Missouri as a constituent of dolomitic limestone or as a vein and cavity filling in the rocks of the Joplin mining district and as a lining in cavities in the dolomitic limestones of the southern and eastern parts of the state.

Dolomite when *powdered* (by scraping the surface of the specimen, for dolomite is softer than steel or glass) effervesces freely in cold dilute hydrochloric (muriatic) acid, but the lump dolomite effervesces *very slowly, if at all.* Calcite effervesces freely in the lump with cold dilute acid. This acid test is the one certain test for dolomite, and works with the thick-bedded formations as well as with the showy, crystal-faced material from veins. See page 11.

Dolomite crystals have a pearly luster and are usually pale pink in the Joplin district. Their faces are commonly curved but where broken show glistening to pearly cleavage faces. These properties assume more significance in mineral determination as one becomes familiar with mineral collections, but the non-technical person can rely on the acid test.

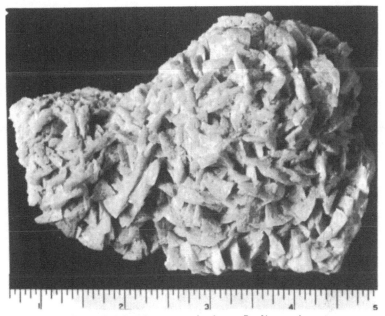

Typical dolomite crystals from Joplin region.

With the above information in mind, one may proceed with certainty to identify a layer of dolomite from a quarry or hillside, or a crystal of it in a hand specimen. First, determine that it is scratched readily with a knife blade or iron nail. Anything too hard to be scratched by steel is neither calcite nor dolomite. Second, scrape a small mound of powder on the lump specimens. Third, apply one or two drops of cold dilute acid to the lump near the powder and allow the acid to run into the powder. If the *lump* effervesces *freely* the specimen is *calcite* mineral or limestone rock. If the *lump* does *not effervesce freely* but the *powder does*, it is *dolomite* mineral or dolomite rock, dolomitic limestone. If neither lump nor powder effervesce it is neither calcite (ordinary limestone) nor dolomite (dolomitic limestone). In the latter case, it may be gypsum, barite, shale, weathered chert, clay, or fire clay, or other rock.

The composition of dolomite is calcium-magnesium carbonate, $CaMg(CO_3)_2$, and when pure runs about 54½ per cent calcium carbonate and 45½ per cent magnesium carbonate. However, dolomite is *not* a *mechanical mixture* of the two carbonates; it is a single crystalline compound wherein the calcium and magnesium are securely interlocked within the arrangement of the atoms. For that reason, the extraction of magnesium metal or other magnesium compounds from dolomite is so difficult and costly that other magnesium minerals, although not nearly so abundant and accessible to industry as dolomite, have been processed to obtain the lightweight metal magnesium.

The thick beds of Missouri dolomitic limestone (and some fairly pure dolomite) have been used chiefly as agricultural stone for soil sweetening, for building stone, gravel, and other purposes to which rough stone is put.

Shale

Shale is a compressed, and layered or laminated clay or mud rock. Consequently it will return to mud if it is wetted with water and rubbed. This may serve as a test for shale. It may occur in thick layers or formations, five, ten to fifty or more feet in thickness, and it ranges downward to paper-thin partings between beds of limestone. It is also commonly associated with coal beds. The color

Shale bluff at a strip mine near Columbia.

of shale varies from light gray to black, or it may be tan, yellow, red, rust, purplish, or green. It is platy, and these thin plates or laminae, piled on each other, make up the shale bed.

Hand specimen of shale shown in preceding picture. Note the characteristic thin layering or lamination.

Some shales are hard, tough, and strong enough to serve as temporary mine roofs. Hard shales are sometimes called "slate" but this name is technically incorrect. *True slate* is a metamorphic rock, composed chiefly of the mineral mica in very fine flakes, and will resist the action of water (weathering) for a long time. Therefore, it is a good roofing material for buildings, whereas shale is composed chiefly of clay minerals, and despite the strength and compactness of the more "slaty" varieties soon disintegrates in water. Missouri "slaty" shale would not serve as satisfactory roofing material.

The red "burned" shale found on burned-out coal mine dumps is called "shale" locally. It is, of course, shale which has been fired more or less to the condition of building brick by the hot burning waste coal. The same original shale could be crushed, molded into brick, "burned" in a kiln, and become a satisfactory building brick. The "burned shale" of the coal mine dumps is used in many places as a drive-way covering.

"Soapstone" is a name applied by some persons to some soft, slippery to greasy shales, but this name is incorrect in a technical sense. True soapstone is a metamorphic rock (shale is sedimentary) which is composed chiefly of the mineral talc. Soapstone occurs abundantly in certain parts of the Appalachian Mountains but is exceedingly sparse in Missouri.

The chief commercial uses of shale are in the manufacture of common brick, building brick, building tile, drain tile, sewer pipe, Portland cement, and other ceramic products. Many shale beds and occurrences are technically suitable for these uses but have no real commercial value because other necessary factors are lacking. In order to make brick, tile, or cement there must be sufficient fuel available at low cost, low-priced bulk transportation of the raw and finished products, available labor, capital for the erection of a plant, and above all a large near-by, dependable market for the manufactured product. The value of a shale deposit, therefore, depends as much upon outside conditions as upon the properties of the rock (shale) itself.

The shales of Missouri were formed from deposits of mud that settled out in sea water which in the past covered this state. Fossil remains of sea-living organisms which are preserved in the shale give evidence of the marine conditions once existent here. Like the muds that are accumulating along the Atlantic coast and in the Gulf of Mexico, where the Mississippi River is discharging its load of silt and clay, so did mud form layers on the bottom of geologically ancient interior seas. In some cases sand was later washed in and covered the mud; in other cases limestone-forming material (like off the coast of Florida today) was deposited on top of the mud. The weight of the overlying beds and the slow movement which raised the sea bottom up to land squeezed out the excess water, compressed and compacted the muds into thin layers, and brought about the shale rock which is exposed to us today.

Soft, easily eroded bed of shale between two more resistant beds of limestone near Columbia.

Black muds, rich in humus and other organic material, formed black shales; red and yellow clays colored by red and yellow iron oxides (iron rusts) formed red and yellow shales; and sandy muds were compacted into gritty, sandy shales. All of them were derived from eroding land and soils just as today our eroding soils contribute to the formation of more shale now in the long, slow process of formation.

The chemical composition of an average shale is not simple, as is shown by the subjoined composite analyses of sedimentary rocks taken from U. S. Geological Survey Professional Paper No. 127.

	78 shales	253 sandstones	345 limestones
SiO_2	58.11	78.31	5.19
Al_2O_3	15.40	4.76	.81
Fe_2O_3	4.02	1.08	.54
FeO	2.45	.30	
M_nO	2.44	1.16	7.89
CaO	3.10	5.50	42.57
Na_2O	1.30	.45	.05
K_2O	3.24	1.32	.33
H_2O+	3.66	1.32	.56
H_2O-	1.33	.31	.21
CO_2	2.63	5.04	41.54
TiO_2	.65	.25	.06
P_2O_5	.17	.08	.04
SO_3	.65	.07	.05
Organic carbon	.80	—	—
	100.	100.	100. approx.

Many persons upon learning that average shale, and even "clay dirt," may contain 15% alumina, Al_2O_3 (equivalent to almost 8% metallic aluminum), become thoughtlessly and erroneously enthusiastic about aluminum ore possibilities on their farms or properties. The aluminum is there all right, but it is so securely combined with silica and other elements that the cost of extraction is now greater than the price of aluminum obtained from less abundant ores. Until chemists find a method of extraction of the metal from ordinary clay or shale that can be carried out at considerably less expense than is now possible, the vast quantities of clay and shale on the earth's surface must be considered a distant reserve of a prohibitively high cost aluminum.

Missouri possesses a little bauxitic clay in the southeastern part of the state but unfortunately does not contain deposits of high grade bauxite, the chief ore of alumium, and so does not contribute to the aluminum production of the United States (see the discussion under DIASPORE CLAY). Arkansas is a leading producer of bauxite, but the geological conditions present in that bauxite locality are so different from Missouri geology that little hope is held for finding bauxite in Missouri, except possibly in the extreme southeastern part.

Fire Clay

Fire clay resembles shale in that it is also a clayey rock and becomes muddy upon wetting and rubbing. It differs from shale at sight in that it (fire clay) is not laminated like shale, but occurs instead in a massive structure which is relatively uniform throughout. Fire clay fractures naturally into blocky or irregular fragments ranging in size from boulders to rough flakes, whereas shale weathers into layered, platy chips.

Shales are commonly buff, yellow, reddish, greenish, or brown in addition to gray in color, whereas good useable fire clay predominates in white, cream, and gray to almost black (if much organic matter is contained in it). Shale is ordinarily gritty with hard sand particles, but most good Missouri fire clay contains only a small amount of sand. Of course, fire clay may grade into sandstone through a sandy clay phase, but this part would not be confused with a layered, gritty shale.

The really determining characteristic of fire clay is its resistance to melting under high temperature. The most positive test for this property is to heat the fire clay to a white heat in comparison with standard preparations (Pyrometric Test Cones) whose fusion temperatures are known. Most of Missouri fire clay will withstand a clean oxidizing heat of over 3000° Fahrenheit without melting.

Clay minerals originate, in general, from the weathering of previously existing silicate rocks and have therefore been called, on occasions, "rotted rocks." The writer has long insisted that clays, particularly fire clays, should be thought of instead as purified or refined rocks. The original silicate rocks and minerals, which were rich in constituents melting at low temperatures, have been soaked, leached, and washed by chemically active ground water and rain water until many of the undesirable elements have been carried away, leaving a refined material which we use and know as fire clay. Missouri possesses one of the largest reserves of finest quality fire clay in the world. Special bulletins on Missouri fire clay are published by the State Geologist, Rolla, Missouri, and may be obtained from his office.

Persons who have undeveloped fire clay deposits on their property frequently ask advice on whom to contact and how to arrange

Plastic fire clay. Shows typical break and naturally polished slicken-sided surfaces. From Mexico, Missouri.

for sale of their fire clay, with the expectation of a fair return and fair treatment. The writer recommends in such cases that the owner of the clay dig into his deposit to obtain a fresh, clean, *representative* specimen of his fire clay (about one pound) and send it to one or more of the large substantial fire brick or refractories companies operating in Missouri. Obviously the company located nearest the deposit, or with the lowest-cost shipping facilities, will be in a favored position to purchase the clay. If the individual is skeptical about the trustworthiness of the company's report, he may send opposite parts of the sample lumps to competitive companies. Of course, the individual may have his clay tested by an independent laboratory at his own expense, but this is ordinarily a useless, costly experience because a company will duplicate those tests in its own laboratory before purchasing the clay. If the refractories companies find the clay useful to them they will proceed with negotiations. If the clay is of inferior quality or if it is not needed by the particular company at *that time*, even though of acceptable quality, usually the company will return a truthful report at no cost to the clay owner.

The same general advice is given in regard to the development of any mineral deposit which the holder may have. The caution about obtaining a representative sample is especially to be emphasized. It applies to the metallic ores, mineral water, and common rock as well as to fire clay.

Plastic Fire Clay

Plastic fire clay forms a sticky, soft mass when wetted and kneaded with water, and will bond together other clays or rocks. Large plastic fire clay deposits occur in Audrain, Callaway, and St. Louis counties, and lesser quantitles are known in Boone, Osage, Gasconade, and Phelps counties. The larger deposits assume a blanket shape with a highly irregular lower surface.

Flint Fire Clay

Flint fire clay is very fine-grained, smooth or slick, and breaks with a shell-like (conchoidal) fracture. It varies in color from white to black, but most flint fire clay mined is near to white. It is relatively non-plastic—that is, does not readily slake or form a sticky mass when worked a little in water. In fact, flint fire clay has been used locally as road surfacing because it does not become very muddy and sticky. Of course, it is inferior to black-top or concrete road surfaces and has too high a commercial value now to be used extensively as road metal.

A hard, white variety of flint fire clay which breaks with numerous conchoidal fractures in appropriate shaped fragments has been called locally "pop-corn flint." This clay, and other sand-free flint clay, when crushed between one's teeth "goes to water" in the mouth. Many clay miners use the chewing test to establish the freedom of their clays from gritty sand, which renders flint clay inferior in quality.

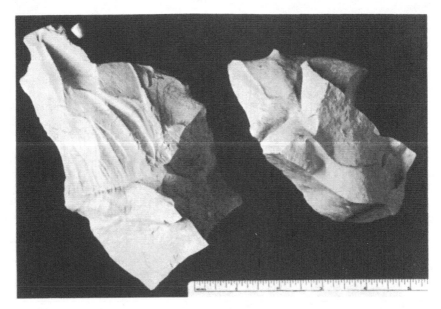

Flint fire clay showing typical "slick break" and conchoidal fracture, from near New Florence.

Flint fire clays occur geologically in old land depressions and in roughly funnel-shaped pits surrounded by an enclosing layer of sandstone, the whole lying within limestone country rock. The most prominent flint fire clay deposits are found in Callaway, Warren, Lincoln, Osage, Gasconade, Maries, Franklin, and Phelps counties.

Diaspore Clay

Diaspore clay is a harsh, usually porous, earthy type of clay which has been found in Warren, Osage, Gasconade, Maries, Franklin, Phelps, and Crawford counties in Missouri. Some diaspore clay is mealy, or finely granular, some is chalky to compact, and much of it is more or less oolitic. Oolites (oolitic structure) are small rounded bodies varying in size from about bird shot to BB shot size, and those in diaspore may be solid or hollow. Their hollow structure contributes to the porous condition in diaspore clay. See page 29.

It is almost impossible to write a description of diaspore clay which can be used to determine it because the clay has so few individual characteristics. A person familiar with diaspore clay, however, can recognize it at a glance. Probably diaspore clay will not be found outside the counties listed above, and within those counties many persons know the clay from contact with the commercial production of it.

Diaspore clay, over 70% alumina, from near Belle.

Diaspore clay occurs in old sink-hole, funnel-shaped pits which formed in the dolomite (limestone) underlying that region. A sandstone layer which lines the pit and commonly stands somewhat above the level of the clay because of the sandstones superior resistance to weathering is known as the "rim rock" of the pit. The diaspore clay may be thought of as an extra-refined type of fire clay from which silica has been leached during prolonged solution in swamps and ground water and the more stable alumina (Al_2O_3) left behind as the refined product.

Pits in the diaspore region may contain from a few truck loads of clay to over 50,000 tons of it, but a pit which produces 10,000 tons of good clay is a valuable and not very common deposit. A small fortune falls to the landowner who finds a large diaspore deposit (pit) on his farm, for royalty rates at this time are not less than $1.00 per ton for first grade, 70% Al_2O_3 clay.

Because of the high value of diaspore, a highly competitive prospecting, leasing, mining, and brokerage business has developed in the diaspore region. Practically all of the thrills, hopes, disappointments, and good fortunes that are associated with oil booms are found in this business and clay area; clay pits are only smaller in scale than wild oil gushers. Clay scouts work in secret, mining leases are contested in court, rumors fly fast in English, German, and German-Swiss over the country telephones, prospecting results may be hidden, personal pressure may be brought to influence a deal, and speedy salesmanship is employed when an exciting find is in the offing. When the legends, traditions, and facts of the diaspore region are collected and recorded, an interesting and essential part of Missouri history will have been written.

Missouri has the only locality in the entire world where relatively pure diaspore clay is now mined in commercial quantities. Because of its extreme resistance to fusion under very high temperatures, diaspore has been called the "aristocrat of fire clays." Diaspore contains a higher percentage of aluminum than does bauxite, the chief ore of aluminum, but because of diaspore's extremely refractory nature it is less easily reduced to aluminum metal than is bauxite, and therefore finds a more specialized use in the manufacture of refractory and super-refractory brick and tile which may even be used in furnaces to calcine aluminum ore. Where resistance to very high temperature has been required, diaspore super fire brick has been remarkably useful.

Burley Clay

Burley clay is a fire clay intermediate in alumina content between flint clay and first quality diaspore. It takes its name from the oolites (rounded pellets of diaspore) which are scattered through a

Burley clay. Note the oolitic structure, the "burls." From a diaspore pit near Swiss.

flint clay base and which were called "burls" by the early clay miners. As the relative number of diaspore oolites increase, an otherwise flint clay becomes burley-flint, then typical burley, and finally grades into second quality and first quality diaspore. Clay in any stage of the variation may be found in some part of the diaspore region or pits. Most of the remarks written on diaspore apply as well to burley clay.

Sandstone

Sandstone is a rock made of sand-size particles more or less well cemented. It is recognized by the grains of sand which are dislodged or scratched loose when the rock is broken, or when scraped with a piece of steel or another hard rock. The old-fashioned grindstone is a sandstone nicely cemented by nature.

Sandstone bluff near mine entrance, Crystal City. (Photo courtesy of Pittsburgh Plate Glass Company.)

Sandstone occurs in thin layers to thick massive beds and deposits which may exceed fifty feet in thickness. In addition to possessing horizontal bedding and parallel bedding planes, some sandstone displays beautiful, intricate cross-bedding or cross-lamination.

The grains of sand composing the stone may be either angular or rounded. They may sparkle in the light from reflections from their crystal faces, or they may have dull, frosted surfaces. Sandstones are ordinarily nearly white in color except where the grains are covered with coatings of yellow or red iron oxide (rust).

The grains themselves are predominantly particles of the mineral quartz, although any rock or mineral of sand size may be present in sandstone. The quartz (see discussion of quartz on page 41)

Cross-bedding in sandstone north of Fredericktown.

Sandstone in hand specimen. Mag-   Quartz sand grains. Magnification
nification 4x.   21x.

may have been derived from pre-existing sandstones or more directly from granite, porphyry, or other igneous rocks in which quartz crystallized when the hot liquid rock solidified. Today quartz grains which are weathering out of igneous rocks and sandstones are being carried by the Missouri river and tributaries to the Mississippi river and thence to the ocean, where extensive deposits of sand are accumulating, probably destined to become widespread beds of sandstone.

The grains of sand may be broken and become angular during their long trip to the ocean, or they may become rounded by rubbing against each other. If they exist in sand dunes, blown about by the wind before being cemented into rock, the grains usually become somewhat rounded. Even after sandstones are buried beneath other rocks, silica, which is carried in solution by ground waters percolating through the sandstone, may crystallize out on the sand grains and restore some brilliant, angular crystal faces to the otherwise rounded grains.

Cementation of loose sand to more or less firm sandstone is due to the presence of clay, iron oxides, or calcite (mineral of limestone) which may be deposited with the sand. All of these cements are softer and weaker than quartz, thereby being broken first and freeing the harder quartz when the rock is scratched or crushed.

A variety of very hard sandstone called quartzite is one that is so strongly cemented that it breaks through the sand grains instead of around them as is the case with ordinary sandstone. This condition is brought about by their being cemented with silica (chemically the same as quartz), which makes for essentially uniform hardness throughout the rock.

Quartzites are, as previously noted, extremely hard, and resist abrasion and chemical weathering. Reddish quartzite boulders occur rather abundantly north of the Missouri River in the glacial clay, sand, and gravel which overlie the sedimentary rocks that form the bed rock or country rock there. Locally, the hard, red quartzite boulders may be called "red niggerheads", although the term "niggerhead" is more often applied to black or dark greenish black boulders of basalt (see page 48) also present in the glacial drift. It is to be recalled that the distinguishing hardness of quartzite is due to the hardness of the quartz grains plus the equal hardness of the silica cement.

Asphaltic sandstone is a sandstone impregnated with a bituminous residue from the evaporation of petroleum which once occupied the pores of the rock. It has been reported from more than a dozen counties in western Missouri, but the most extensive deposits are probably in Barton, Vernon, and Lafayette counties.

Attention has been directed to the origin of sandstones from ocean deposits of sand and from sand dunes, but it should be recognized also that river channels and stream valleys which contain deposits of sand (such as those on floodplains, river bottoms, and sand bars) may be covered, and the sand consolidated to sandstone. Many years ago, even long ago geologically, a large river, almost comparable in size to the Missouri river, occupied a channel which is now represented by a long narrow sandstone deposit extending from a little north of Clinton through Warrensburg to Lexington and then east through Moberly almost to Paris. Smaller channel sandstones are abundant in other areas in Missouri.

The sandstones of the so-called Roubidoux formation, which occurs in south central Missouri, commonly show well-preserved ripple marks on the rock slabs. These marks were formed exactly as their name suggests—in sand which was thrown into ripples by the shallow water in which it accumulated and was covered and cemented so as to retain the ripple forms.

Ripple marks in limy sandstone.

Sandstone is used for building stone, walks, grindstones, furnace linings, and rock gardens. Large quantities are mined each year near Pacific, Festus and Crystal City, Klondike, and Hermann, for the manufacture of glass and other uses. Common glass is a cooled melt of relatively pure silica sand, soda ash, and lime. Asphaltic sandstone is used in road building. Sand-lime brick are made of sand. Sand is used as a molding material for metal castings, a parting substance between brick in kilns, and in large quantities in concrete and mortar mixtures.

Chert, Flint

The names chert and flint have in some regions been used for the same hard, fine-grained rock found so abundantly in Missouri, but correct usage employs chert for the white and gray varieties, and flint for the black variety. Flint may be thought of as slightly impure chert, a chert which is colored black by a small amount of pigment, usually fine carbon, or perhaps iron sulphide, scattered through it like fine dust.

Chert is characterized by being harder than glass, brittle, very fine-grained, and by breaking with a smooth, rounded or hollowed clam shell-like (conchoidal) fracture and sharp edges. It was used

Chert, fossiliferous and slightly speckled. Note typical sharp edges, smooth surfaces, and conchoidal fracture. From near Columbia.

by Indians to make arrow heads. It accumulates in abundance both in stream beds as gravel which has been more or less rounded by wear, and on the hillsides within the soil and sub-soil. Yellow and red iron oxides may stain and penetrate weathered chert gravel so that it becomes reddish, rusty, tan, yellow or brown.

Chert remains abundant because of its extreme resistance to weathering. It is so hard that stream action wears it only very slowly. Its chemical composition is silica, SiO_2, a substance which is but little affected chemically by ground water. Where chert has contained fine grains of calcite scattered through it, the calcite may be removed in solution, leaving pores, and a zone of porous, light weight, tripolitic chert, harsh to the feel and enveloping an unaltered interior (See WEATHERED CHERT). Not uncommonly, fossil remains of calcite which were embedded in chert have been dissolved, leaving their hollow impressions.

Chert in Missouri originally occurs chiefly in limestone formations, where it is found as nodules, lenses, stringers, and irregular forms in and between the limestone beds. Chert and flint may be deposited directly from silica in solution, or they may replace (substitute for) wood, fossils, or older rock where silica-bearing solutions contact and react with the replaced substance. For example, petrified wood usually is wood which has been replaced molecule by molecule with silica. This statement applies equally to the brightly colored petrified wood in the Petrified Forest in Arizona and to that with comparatively drab coloring in Missouri. Many other siliceous fossils, notably animal remains, are replacements of calcite (limestone) by silica.

In anticipation that the reader may have difficulty understanding how silica may go into solution if chert (silica) is hardly attacked by the weathering process, it should be explained that silica is freed in solution predominately during the weathering of complex silica-combinations, silicates, rather than from uncombined silica. For instance, feldspar and pyroxene from granite or gabbro weather in ground water to a soil-forming clay mineral and release some silica in solution in the ground water. After this silica is redeposited in an uncombined form, like chert, it becomes highly insoluble.

An observation in regard to flint is that the metallic "flints" which are used to ignite gas burners or cigarette lighters are not black chert, SiO_2. Instead, they are special alloys containing rather uncommon elements which possess the useful characteristic of emitting a brilliant hot spark when harshly scratched.

Chert is the chief source of natural gravel in Missouri because it accumulates in stream beds and on hillsides on account of its resistance to weathering. The piles of "chats" in the Joplin region, containing thousands of tons of crushed chert, have been used in part in road surfacing material.

Weathered Chert

Weathered chert, or leached chert, is a white to gray, or yellowish, porous, light-weight, harsh to feel, chalky-appearing rock which occurs over much of the southern half of Missouri. It does not effervesce in acid. Usually it occurs as a zone from a fraction of, to more than an inch in thickness, about a denser core of hard, compact chert (flint), or makes up an entire small rock fragment or gravel.

Chert hand specimen showing quartz-lined fossil cavity in center, compact fresh chert in interior, and chalky-appearing weathered outside margins. From near Columbia.

It develops as a relatively insoluble residue left when the more soluble rock material in association has been leached away during the weathering process. Its composition approaches pure silica. It has no established use and no commercial value.

"Kaoleen"

"Kaoleen" is a term used locally in part of south-central Missouri to refer to a chalky, white to tan or buff, porous weathered chert, but the name should be dropped because it is unnecessary (use weathered chert), confusing, and not recognized elsewhere. Most probably the term arose in corruption of the word *kaolin,* which is the name for a true, high-quality clay, to which the leached and weathered chert bears a slight resemblance. Kaolin has the chemical composition of clay (hydrous aluminum silicate), whereas "kaoleen" is impure silica. See the discussion on Weathered Chert.

Tripoli

Tripoli occurs in the vicinity of Seneca, Newton County, Missouri. It is a light-weight, porous, white to creamy, siliceous rock, which may be scratched because of its softness. Tripoli represents the porous insoluble residue of an earlier rock, which was composed of skeletal insoluble silica and interstitial soluble calcium carbonate (calcite), the latter having been dissolved away by ground water. Tripoli has a chalky appearance but is totally unlike chalk chemically. Tripoli is nearly pure silica, whereas chalk is calcium carbonate. Any tripoli-like rock found in Missouri outside the region of tripoli mines is likely to be a fragment of weathered chert which is described above.

Tripoli has been used as an abrasive, a polishing agent, a parting material in molding sand, and a filter rock.

Agate

Agate is a banded variety of chert. Although the chemical composition of agate is SiO_2, the same as chert, a microscopically fibrous part of it having a waxy luster or varying in color or translucency may give the appearance to the rock that we associate with the name agate. The mineral name chalcedony is given to the fibrous, waxy material.

Typical agates are most abundant in Missouri in the glacial and stream gravels in the northern part of the state, although part of the Potosi drusy quartz and chalcedony in the southeast is also prized. The large gravel pit near LaGrange, in the northeast, has furnished many beautiful specimens, not only of agate, but also of petrified wood and fossils.

Missouri lapidists and collectors of semi-precious stones find plenty of interesting raw material within their own state.

Jasper

Jasper is chert which is colored red or yellowish brown by iron oxides.

Granite

Granite is a granular (coarse-grained) rock whch has a glassy luster and is too hard to be scratched appreciably by steel. It may be white to gray, tan, brown, or pink to red in color, but pinkish to red granite predominates in Missouri. Some black stone, referred to locally as "black granite," is usually a variety of gabbro. Most Missouri granite is coarse-grained, so that the constituent mineral grains—quartz, feldspar, and (less frequently) mica—can be readily recognized by anyone familiar with those minerals. It makes up many

Close view of a granite hand specimen. Feldspar predominates. Quartz appears dark in the photograph, but shows glistening edges and points. From Graniteville.

of the mountains and hills in Iron, Madison, and St. Francois counties and adjacent regions. North of the Missouri River, or where the glacial deposits remain, granite boulders may occur in the sandy and clayey glacial drift.

The mineral quartz is recognized in granite by its glistening, oily luster, really more brilliant than the luster of glass, and by its curved to irregular broken surface. Furthermore, the brilliant luster of quartz is not dulled by exposure to weather.

The mineral feldspar, in granite, has a glassy luster on the tiny flat cleavage faces where the individual grains are broken. Where weathered, feldspar becomes dulled, and chalky to dusty or clayey. Fresh feldspar may be glassy, white, buff, pink, red, in intermediate shades in color. With the mica, it imparts most of the color to granite.

Mica is recognized by its softness and its ability to be split very easily into tiny flakes. Other minerals may be found in granite under the microscope, but they have little importance or significance.

Granite is an intrusive igneous rock; that is, it solidified from a hot liquid state (like lava) in a large body, beneath, or surrounded by pre-existing rocks. Because of slow solidification a coarse-grained texture was developed. In southeastern Missouri where granite is now exposed at the surface (for example, the Elephant Rocks State Park at Graniteville), that granite was covered originally by hun-

Granite at the "Elephant Rocks," Graniteville. The large boulders now rounded by weathering are remnants of a higher part of the large granite body which underlies this region. (Photograph courtesy of Mr. Noel Hubbard).

dreds of feet of rock at the time it solidified from a liquid. During the millions of years which have elapsed since the granite solidified, its cover and the upper part of the granite have been eroded away by streams and rain after weathering to soil material. In fact, the ocean has covered the area several times during its long geological history.

Missouri has a fine quality of granite in large quantity in southeastern Missouri. Granite is used for building, structural and monument purposes (see discussion under marble), for rubble stone, riprap, ballast, gravel, paving blocks, crushed chicken gravel, and for other specialized uses where favorably located. Chemical analyses of granite and porphry, taken from Missouri Geological Survey Report, Volume VIII, 1895, follow.

	Porphyry 6 miles east of Ironton	Granite 6 miles east of Ironton
SiO_2	71.88	72.35
Al_2O_3	12.88	13.78
Fe_2O_3	3.05	1.87
FeO	1.05	0.36
CaO	1.13	0.87
MgO	0.33	0.42
K_2O	4.46	4.49
Na_2O	4.21	4.14
P_2O_5	0.15	0.13
TiO_2	0.22	0.44
Ignition loss	0.26	0.54

The glacial granite boulders found in central to northern Missouri also solidified as intrusive rock in the northern United States or in Canada. After being exposed at the surface they were picked up and carried down by the geogically recent, continental ice sheet (glacier) that moved down from Canada to across the northern half of Missouri. Scratches and grooves may have been cut in some of these boulders, or flat faces scoured and planed off as they were scraped against other hard rocks. Quartz gravel is usually present, often in abundance, in glacial deposits. Small specimens of native metallic copper, which come from near Lake Superior, have been found in Missouri glacial deposits. Even diamonds from an unknown source in the north were carried by the ice down into the United States. The history of the glaciation is a spectacular account of changes which our continent has undergone in the geological past.

Glacial scratches on boulder carried by the large glacier in northern Missouri long ago. Boulder from near Columbia.

Quartz

Quartz is a mineral of wide-spread occurrence which is characterized by the following properties: (1) it is considerably harder than glass or steel, (2) it has a high luster, glassy to oily, (3) it breaks with an irregular or rough glistening fracture, and (4) it crystallizes in six-sided crystals when it grows unobstructed. Ordinary acids do not attack quartz, and it is relatively unaffected by chemical weathering in Missouri. Its composition is silicon dioxide, SiO_2.

Quartz occurs in granite as the lustrous, partially rounded grains which constitute perhaps 20% of the rock (feldspar makes up most of the more opaque remainder which breaks with many small flat faces), and is recognized in the small glistening grains in the porphyry. Hence it is an important igneous rock-forming mineral.

Sandstone in Missouri is made almost entirely of quartz grains which have been broken, worn, and more or less rounded during their long travel history. The sandstone formation quarried and mined near Pacific and Crystal City, named the St. Peter sandstone formation, is an outstandingly pure quartz sandstone and therefore usable in the glass industry. It is obvious that quartz is an important constituent of sedimentary rocks.

Lustrous, translucent quartz. The irregular fracture and oily luster are characteristic.

Further, in the sedimentary dolomite formation near Potosi, fine to coarse quartz crystals line the surfaces of cavities and pockets in the stone. This cavity coating of quartz which reflects light brilliantly from the many small crystal faces is called drusy quartz by the mineralogist, but is locally and popularly known as "blossom rock." Thousands of pounds of "blossom rock" are sold each year for rock gardens and various ornamental purposes.

In northeastern Missouri quartz crystals line the hollow, more or less spherical bodies called Geodes, which vary in size from small nuts to melons, and weather out of the so-called Warsaw formation. Other types of hollow cavities in many Missouri rocks may contain quartz growing inward from their walls.

Missouri chert is composed primarily of quartz in microscopically fine grains; likewise, agate and petrified wood may contain abundant quartz. Other varieties are rock crystal, rose quartz, amethyst, false topaz, bloodstone, carnelian, and onyx.

Quartz crystallized in an igneous rock as the hot fluid cooled through its "freezing" temperature interval, which was probably not below 1000°F. In the cases of the quartz in geodes, the drusy quartz, or that in cavities within petrified wood, quartz crystals grew from ground water solutions which must have carried very low concentrations of silica in solution, and whose temperatures did not depart far from that of rocks buried at various depths today. Although quartz is a very common and abundant mineral, our specific knowledge about its transport and deposition is surprisingly meager.

Quartz crystal cluster.   Crystals are six-sided.   From Arkansas.

Quartz crystals are used in large quantities in radio apparatus where it is necessary to maintain very close control on the tuning of a circuit. This use requires quartz of highest quality and crystals above minimum size, which have never been found in Missouri and probably are not present. Silica production from this state is in its sandstone, tripoli, chert chats, and rock garden ornamental stone.

Feldspar

Feldspar is a white to pink or red mineral having a glassy luster on its flat broken surfaces (cleavage faces). It will scratch window glass.

It is the most abundant mineral in granite and usually controls the color of that rock; for example, the red granite at Graniteville contains red feldspar, and the pink-gray granite in the Knoblick region has feldspar of those colors. Small bodies or bands of very coarse feldspar, quartz, and mica (pegmatite dikes) which cut the granite may contain crystals of feldspar large enough to be recovered as small, hand specimens, but otherwise it does not occur in coarse fragments. The recognizable crystals, or phenocrysts, in the porphyry are mainly feldspar.

A large piece of feldspar showing cleavage surfaces.

Feldspar is really a family name for a group of several minerals, all of which are crystallized in the igneous rocks. The potassium (potash)-containing varieties, named orthoclase and microcline, occur in the granite and porphyry, whereas plagioclase, a calcium-sodium (lime-soda) feldspar is in gabbro, diabase, and basalt.

Plagioclase commonly has a thin, lath shape, is a shade of gray, and makes up the lighter colored part of the greenish to dark gray igneous rocks. Further differences between it and orthoclase may interest the mineralogist but are of little concern to the non-technical person.

Pulverized feldspars are used extensively in the ceramic industries, but Missouri does not have any productive deposits. Under natural, long-time weathering processes feldspar usually decomposes to clay which may be used technically, but the usual fate of it is soil formation.

Mica

Mica, incorrectly called isinglass, is an elastic, fairly soft, platy mineral, which may be split into flakes of paper thinness. The relatively clear variety is called muscovite, and the brownish black to black variety is biotite, both being members of the mica family. They may occur in Missouri in small grains in the igneous rocks, except that muscovite may be present in sandstone, where it was deposited along with the quartz sand.

Mica is used chiefly as insulating material in the electrical industry where large sheets are required. Another use is as window or chimney material in stoves or lanterns. Missouri has no mica which is satisfactory for these purposes.

Porphyry, Rhyolite, Rhyolite Porphyry

Porphyry and granite are the two most abundant igneous rocks in southeastern Missouri (Iron, Madison, and St. Francois counties, and adjacent country). The porphyry there is a compact, very fine-grained, almost glassy, hard, brittle rock that varies in color from light gray through pink and red to dark purplish red and almost black. It always breaks with a horny, flinty fracture. Small mineral crystals of glistening quartz and usually reddish feldspar are generally scattered throughout the dense background (groundmass). The cry-

Rhyolite porphyry showing phenocrysts (light "freckles") of quartz and feldspar. From near Ironton.

stals are commonly about one-sixteenth of an inch in cross section and ordinarily constitute from about ten to twenty per cent of the rock. Other names, somewhat more specific than simple porphyry, which are applied technically to certain phases of the rock are rhyolite, and rhyolite porphyry.

The porphyry of southeastern Missouri is igneous rock which in the main poured out as lava flows, millions of years ago. Volcanic dust or "ash" was erupted during the same period, and layers of it, now strongly cemented, are found in association with the flow rock.

The Missouri rhyolite porphyry has about the same chemical composition (see page 40) as Missouri granite, but whereas granite is coarse-grained, the porphyry has an extremely fine-grained to almost glassy ground-mass. This difference in texture (grain size) is due to the difference in rate of solidification. The porphyry lava flows chilled and solidified very rapidly, thereby freezing the liquid to glassy and extremely fine-grained rock, except for the scattered larger crystals (phenocrysts) which had developed prior to eruption. Granite, on the other hand, solidified very slowly under a thick cover of rock which acted as a heat insulator, and during the long time of solidification large or coarse grains of minerals could grow and develop by crystallization so that a coarse-textured rock (granite) was formed.

The relative ages of the Missouri igneous rocks are of interest to geologists and to most persons who recognize the different types within a small area. It has been found that the prophyry was invaded by the granitic liquid, that both the porphyry and granite were cracked after solidification, and that liquid basalt rose and filled the cracks. Hence the porphyry is the oldest, the granite next in age, and the basalt is youngest. In fact, it may be mentioned in passing that some basalt and allied dikes have been found cutting through the sedimentary sandstone, shale, and limestone which overlie the igneous granite and porphyry and are much younger.

Missouri porphyry has little use or value other than of bulk or crushed stone.

Basalt

Basalt is a fine-grained, dark-gray, dark-green, or greenish-black rock which is hard enough to be scratched with difficulty by steel. It originated by the solidification of lava. Today, basalt rock is forming where lava at the Hawaiian volcanoes solidifies.

The relatively small amount of basalt in southeastern Missouri solidified mostly in cracks within other rocks through which it rose. Those occurrences—that is, fillings in nearly vertical cracks—are called dikes. The basalt dikes in southeastern Missouri have been exposed by the weathering and erosion of rocks which previously covered them.

A dark dike of basalt in granite near Silver Mines.

In northern Missouri, boulders of basalt may be found in deposits of glacial clay, sand, and gravel (glacial drift), where they were left after the melting of the great ice sheet which brought the basalt down from ancient dikes and igneous bodies cropping out in the northern United States and Canada. Many of the boulders have been rounded by weathering, and their shape, together with their dark color, has stimulated the local name "niggerhead" for them.

Basalt in hand specimen.

Basalt is a strong, tough, well-knit rock that will withstand heavy blows from a sledge hammer, which usually rebounds upon striking. Except for use as rubble stones, basalt has no commercial value. It weathers characteristically to a yellowish, brownish, or reddish surface coating of iron oxide and clay.

Gabbro and Diabase

Gabbro and Diabase are dark-colored, coarse-grained, hard igneous rocks, which may be found in the granite and porphyry regions of southeastern Missouri and as separate boulders in the glacial deposits north of the Missouri River. Both resemble basalt, which has been described in detail elsewhere, except that basalt is fine-grained, whereas gabbro and diabase are coarse-grained (separate grains easily distinguished without a magnifying glass). The layman is

Diabase hand specimen. From near Roselle.

ordinarily not concerned with the technical differences between gabbro and diabase, which appear about the same. Both contain plagioclase feldspar (see FELDSPAR) and a dark green mineral of the pyroxene family.

Gabbro and Diabase are sometimes called "black granite." Their chief use is as bulk or rubble-stone, although special varieties may be used for building purposes.

Coal

Coal is so well known that little need be written about its distinguishing characteristics. Most of the coal in Missouri is of about bituminous rank, although some cannel coal, which is discussed below, is also present.

Missouri bituminous coal occurs in the northern and western parts of the state. It contains bands of dull coal, bands of glistening "glance" coal, the sooty "mineral charcoal," and common mineral impurities like calcite, gypsum, pyrite and marcasite ("sulphur"), clay minerals, and quartz. Bituminous coal breaks with essentially a cubical fracture.

It occurs in horizontal or nearly horizontal beds or "seams," which may be followed considerable distances laterally without necessarily encountering much change. Usually, a fireclay or a fire clay-like under-clay immediately underlies the coal, but the overlying rock (the roof) may be shale (slate? see discussion of SHALE), sandstone, or less commonly, limestone.

Bed of coal exposed by stream erosion, near Columbia.

Coal originates from pre-existing plants and may be thought of as Mother Nature's storage cellar of "preserved" plant life. The Missouri coal began millions of years ago as mosses, tree-like ferns, conifers, and various plants that reproduce by spores, which flourished in great wide-spread swamps. Insects were abundant, as is indicated by their remains. Rain was probably plentiful and climate favorable, so that such vegetation thrived luxuriantly. Today, fallen forest timber of the highland disappears by oxidizing and decaying in the air; but in swamp land the leaves, stems, pollen and woody trunks fall into and under water and under favorable conditions decompose through bacterial and chemical action into layers and pools of slippery, oozy, blackish humic gel (like brownish black gelatin, "jello"), which remains. Likewise, in ages past, more and more plant material continued to live, fall, and accumulate in the old coal swamps until very thick deposits of the woody gel existed.

Eventually land-sea or climatic conditions changed, and plant life died out as mud, sand, or other rock-forming material was swept in to cover, as a lid, the stored-up plant remains. The weight of overlying beds squeezed out excess water from the woody gel, and from the time of covering through the present day, gases (like mine gases), and other volatile constituents of the coal have been given off.

A bed of coal, which consists chiefly of black combustible carbon, with volatile constituents and non-volatile ash substances, has resulted. Man uses the coal by burning it directly, or it may be coked and the volatile constituents recovered in coal tar and other compounds. The mineral impurities like the calcite, gypsum, clay, sand, and brassy pyrite or marcasite, are shaken through the grates as ash or melted as clinkers.

In nature, the pyrite and marcasite minerals may oxidize in ground water percolating over them to form dilute sulphuric acid, the acid mine waters.

Cannel coal in Missouri has been found chiefly in old sink-hole deposits through part of central Missouri. It is characterized by fracturing conchoidally and having a more massive structure (instead of the layered structure common to bituminous coal). Cannel coal burns to a very hot, rather quick fire because of high volatile content, and is thought to have developed from accumulations very rich in plant spores.

Coal mining is an important industry in Missouri, and a special bulletin on coal has been published by the State Geological Survey at Rolla, Missouri.

Pyrite and Marcasite

Pyrite and Marcasite (Fool's gold, "sulphur") are brassy yellow, metallic, heavy minerals whch will scratch glass but which cannot themselves be scratched by a knife, and which will leave a dark-greenish to black mark or streak when rubbed across unglazed porcelain or chert rock. Both are composed of iron sulphide, FeS_2—iron 46.6 per cent, and sulphur 53.4 per cent. Although they have the same chemical composition, they differ in internal atomic and crystalline structure, which is of interest to scientific mineralogists. Pyrite may crystallize in cubes, or in forms called pyritohedrons, named from pyrite, whereas marcasite crystallizes in characteristic arrow-shaped or cockscomb forms. Marcasite weathers a little more readily than does pyrite, but otherwise they are much the same to the casual observer.

Pyrite and marcasite have been called "fool's gold" because so many persons have been fooled, sometimes with serious financial consequences, by their slight resemblance to true gold. True gold is soft, usually slightly orange-yellow in color, malleable, and unaffected by ordinary acids; and it leaves a gold-colored streak when rubbed on unglazed porcelain or a hard white rock. Pyrite, in contrast, is quite hard (harder than steel), is brassy yellow with perhaps

Brassy, granular pyrite in hand specimen.

Pyrite in crystal cubes, and replacement of fossils.

a slight greenish tinge except where tarnished, is brittle, is corroded by acids or oxidizing ground waters, and leaves a greenish black to black streak on a white rock. One readily notices the difference in color between pyrite and gold (such as is in a piece of good quality jewelry), when the two are viewed close together. Yellowish, partially weathered mica has also been mistaken for gold.

Pyrite and marcasite occur abundantly in most of the metal-mining districts of Missouri, as the "brass," or "sulphur balls," etc., in coal, as small nodules or pellets in some limestone, shale and sandstone, as replacements of fossils, and as minute crystals in granite, porphyry, and the other igneous rocks. Several marcasite mines have been developed in old sinkhole deposits in south central Missouri, but these are not in production at the time of this writing. The sinkhole iron mines of south central Missouri contained pyrite-marcasite before oxidation to the iron oxide ore, and some of them still contain the sulphides in their lower levels.

Marcasite weathers (oxidizes) very readily under most conditions, with the formation of (1) yellowish brown iron oxide, the mineral limonite, which may stain rocks, soil, stream bank, etc., and (2) weak sulphuric acid water. The sulphuric acid solution may

Marcasite crystal cluster from Joplin region. The arrowhead or cockscomb crystal form is characteristic of marcasite.

react with more marcasite or pyrite and evolve a gas, hydrogen sulphide, H_2S, which has a rotten-egg odor. This explains the foul odor often noticed around old coal mine dumps. Heat is evolved in these reactions, and coal waste on the dump may be ignited by the heat of the chemical reactions. The burning pyrite, or elemental sulphur, gives off sulphur dioxide, "burning sulphur fumes," which add to the odor and heat around a coal mine dump. The burning coal waste and the chemical reactions may raise the temperature of the coal waste pile high enough to fire or "burn" the shale rock to a red, partially vitrified, natural brick-like material, which is sold or distributed as "coal dump shale" or "burned shale," or "red shale" for all-weather surfacing of drives or walks.

Pyrite and marcasite have been used in the commercial manufacture of sulphuric acid, but elemental sulphur can now be utilized more economically, so that now no market exists for pyrite or marcasite in Missouri. In earlier times only large deposits containing thousands of tons of the mineral had any value. In some foreign countries pyrite is burned and the fumes utilized for the manufacture of sulphuric acid, while the cinder, an iron oxide and iron ore, is smelted to recover metalic iron.

The origin of pyrite and marcasite is as variable as its enclosing rock. No general statement can be made which will include the igneous rock pyrite, the Joplin marcasite, the "sulphur" of the coal, and occurrences in sink holes and various sedimentary rocks. A discussion of all these origins alone would fill a pamphlet as large as this one on Missouri rocks.

Conglomerate

Conglomerate is a rock composed of gravel, pebbles, and boulders cemented together, with more or less sand and clay between the larger fragments. It is truly a conglomeration of rock fragments as one would find loose today in a stream or ocean shore gravel bar, or in a hillside gravel bank. Probably the conglomerate most abundantly exposed in Missouri is that overlying the igneous rocks in the southeast part of the state.

Gneiss

Gneiss is a hard, granular rock which exhibits a coarsely banded structure (resulting from metamorphism). The bands are evident because of color differences due to different mineral content; those dark in color are commonly rich in dark mica (biotite) or hornblende (a dark green to black, hard mineral), whereas the light bands contain feldspar and quartz. Many gneisses have about the same mineral composition as granite; hence, for our nontechnical purposes, a banded rock, otherwise granite-like, is a gneiss.

Gneiss typically banded.

Gneiss is a metamorphic rock, a *changed* rock. The banded structure was developed by a combination of very high pressure, high temperature, and solutions acting on a previously existing rock in essentially a solid condition. The original rock may have been an igneous or sedimentary rock whch has been crushed or made to flow into bands, or has been re-crystalized. The tremendous pressure which operated during the banding of most gneisses also crumpled square miles of rock thousands of feet thick into folded and broken (faulted) mountains. True slates, marbles, and some quartzites are formed from soft shales, limestones, and sandstones, respectively, in the metamorphic process.

Almost no metamorphic rock of this regional type crops out in Missouri, but the boulders of gneiss which are found in the glacial deposits were picked up in Canada or the northern United States and carried to Missouri by a continental glacier thousands of years ago.

Except for use as bulk stone or possible structural purposes the gneiss in Missouri has no value. The glistening yellowish mica sometimes seen in gneiss is not gold, of course, and is likewise valueless.

Hematite

Hematite ("keel") is a heavy, red to purplish red, dull to glistening mineral which leaves a red mark or streak when rubbed on a hard white rock (like chert) or on unglazed porcelain. This

Hematite: glistening, fine-grained, and dark red.

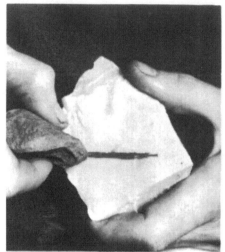

Hematite makes a deep red mark or streak on a hard white rock or unglazed porcelain.

red color of hematite coating or stain is responsible for our red clays, red soils, red iron rust, reddish creek-water, and almost every bit of natural, red mineral matter in Missouri. Hematite is iron oxide, Fe_2O_3, and has a close associate, limonite, which is yellow to brown in color, and has the chemical composition $Fe_2O_3 \cdot nH_2O$. The two are mentioned together here because they are commonly associated in nature, where they can be recognized in mixture by the yellowish red or reddish brown colors on rocks or soils. Individual discussion is given limonite under its heading, but its relationship to hematite is repeated here for obvious reasons.

Hematite varies in hardness enough that some specimens can be scratched easily with iron, whereas others are almost as hard as that metal itself. Where clay occurs mixed with hematite, as in paint ore, it may be quite soft, but "blue kidney ore" is usually hard.

Hematite is the ore (iron ore) mineral at Iron Mountain and Pilot Knob mining districts and in the various sink-hole mines or pits in south central Missouri. Scattered boulders of hematite occur in non-commercial quantities within a shaly layer (lower part of Pennsylvanian age rocks) which crops out extensively in central Missouri, and the finding of these boulders has at times, unfortunately, stimulated short-lived hopes of locating a valuable depost of iron ore. Flaming red soil or mountains of red solid rock (as are present in western United States) may be colored by less than five per cent iron oxide and are in no sense iron ore because the iron is not concentrated. Iron is the fourth most abundant element in the earth's crust, but workable iron mines and deposits are few and far between. To be commercially valuable an iron ore deposit must contain tens of thousands of tons and be relatively free from impurities, notably sulphur and phosphorus. Hence, not many Missouri farms are locations of iron ore deposits.

The origin of Missouri hematite is about as diverse as its occurrences. Hot iron-rich solutions coming from an igneous source below are believed to have introduced the hematite in the Iron Mountain-Pilot Knob area, but the sink-hole hematite resulted from the oxidation of iron sulphide. Weathering of older iron-containing rocks and minerals gave rise to the coloring hematite seen on our sub-soil and surface rock.

Hematite is used as a polishing agent, as a pigment in paint, and, of course, as an ore of metallic iron. In the smelting of iron from hematite the ore is mixed in a huge, chimney-shaped blast furnace with coke (from coal) and limestone. Air is blown into the furnace as into a blacksmith's forge; and the coke and gasses, burning at an incandescent heat, take the oxygen from the Fe_2O_3, leaving metallic iron which melts and is run out of the furnace at periodic intervals. Thus the smelting process is the opposite of the rusting process. The impurities and cinder run out as molten slag.

Limonite

Limonite is a heavy, yellow to brown, or brownish black mineral which always leaves a yellow to brown mark or streak when rubbed across a hard white rock or unglazed porcelain. It usually has a

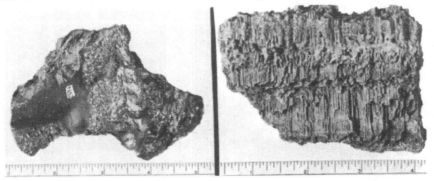

Dark brown limonite.   Stalactitic limonite from southeastern Missouri.

dull luster on a broken surface, and may vary from thumb-nail hardness to almost that of steel. The distinguishing test is its yellow to brown streak.

In composition limonite is iron oxide which contains more or less water chemically combined, $Fe_2O_3 \cdot nH_2O$. That is, it may be dried bone-dry at the temperature of boiling water, but upon heating to redness the additional, chemically held water will be driven off.

Limonite is ordinarily formed from the weathering of other iron-containing minerals (pyrite, for example) and is therefore a wide-spread mineral in surface rock, in films on pools of water, and in soil, all of which it colors yellow to brown. In fact, almost all of the yellow to brown inorganic mineral color and stain seen in nature is that of limonite.

Commercial deposits of limonite occur in southeastern Missouri where large boulders, discontinuous and irregular lenses or beds, pipes, nodules, and gravel to clay-sized particles of the mineral are associated with the cherty, gravelly residual clay. Usually the ore is crushed, hand-sorted, and washed preparatory to concentration for shipment to a furnace or for use in cement manufacture. As in the case of hematite, unless one has a deposit amounting to thousands of tons of ore it has little commercial value, and unless the mineral is relatively pure it can not be used.

Paint Ore or Red Ocher

An intensely red-colored, clayey iron ore has been mined for paint pigment in several deposits in south central Missouri. It occurs in sink hole deposits like those containing fire clay. Brown ocher may be available from southeast Missouri.

Iron Band Diaspore

Shells of red or reddish brown iron oxide occur about cores of diaspore clay in some of those deposits south of the Missouri River. Previously this material had no value, but in the last few years it has been purchased for and shipped to a cement company, which used it in the manufacture of cement. Diaspore clay is discussed elsewhere in this pamphlet.

Manganese Ore

Several manganese minerals make up the manganese ore which occurs to a limited extent in southeast Missouri, principally in Shannon, Reynolds, Carter, Iron, and Madison counties. Although the Missouri manganese minerals are usually heavy, black or nearly so, and have a black or brownish-black mark or streak, the identification of the individual minerals is difficult and should be left to a technically trained mineralogist.

Manganese minerals are used in the chemical industry and in the production of certain kinds of iron. A special report on the manganese deposits of Missouri is available at the Missouri Geological Survey, Rolla, Missouri.

Galena

Galena ("lead") is a heavy, soft, somewhat brittle ore of lead. It has a brilliant metallic luster, and silvery gray color on a freshly broken surface. Where weathered it appears dull gray. It can be scratched with a knife, and breaks with surfaces at 90°, forming cubes. The unbroken, original crystal form of galena which has grown unobstructed in a vein opening is commonly cubical in habit or a modification thereof. It leaves a dark, lead-gray to black mark or streak when rubbed across unglazed porcelain or chert.

A "cube" of galena.   Cluster of galena crystals from Joplin region.

Galena is lead sulphide, PbS, and when pure contains 86.6 per cent lead and 13.4 per cent sulphur. Small amounts of silver may also be present.

Galena commonly occurs in Missouri as a cavity filling in crushed limestone or chert, or as a replacement in limestone or dolomite, or in shale, so that a large quantity of practically worthless enclosing rock (gangue) must be taken out in order to obtain the desired galena. If a person desires to estimate the value of his galena (lead) prospect by having an analysis or assay made of his ore, he must include in his sample the gangue rock that would of necessity have to be taken out when mining his ore. Too often persons carefully select for analysis a choice galena specimen which may run over 80% lead, only to find that as a practical mine product it would be reduced to less than 5% lead in all the rock which also would have to be taken out.

After a galena ore is mined it is customarily crushed and the galena removed from the gangue by a gravity-separation process which takes advantage of the difference in "heaviness" (specific gravity) between galena (7.5) and limestone (calcite) or chert (2.7-2.6), or by a froth flotation process in which the galena is preferentially wetted and carried off by an oily froth or foam. The galena concentrate is roasted to burn out the sulphur, reduced by carbon, and smelted to metallic lead. The origin of some Missouri lead deposits is debatable, but the writer believes the most reasonable explanation to be that warm, chemically active waters arose from an igneous body below and carried to the place of deposition the lead which they held in solution.

Missouri is one of the leading producers of lead in the world from its Flat River, Fredericktown, Joplin, and central Missouri districts, from which in 1941 lead concentrates having a value of over $15,000,000 were produced.

Sphalerite

Sphalerite (locally called Jack, Rosin Jack, Black Jack, Ruby Jack, Zinc, Rosin Spar) is a tan-brown, resinous, brown or brownish black mineral having a very high luster on its broken (cleavage) surfaces. Much of it so strongly resembles lump rosin that the term "Rosin Jack" is truly descriptive. Less commonly, a ruby red variety occurs as crystals perched on other sphalerite or on waste rock. Sphalerite is readily scratched with steel. Its chemical composition is zinc sulphide, ZnS—zinc 67 per cent, sulphur 33 per cent—and it is an important ore of zinc.

Sphalerite occurs abundantly in the mining district of southwest Missouri, but small, non-commercial amounts of it have been found through an area extending even north of the Missouri River. At the mines, after the ore and rock are taken out, they are crushed and separated, the ore going to the smelter and the rock to tailings piles. Under the old milling process employed in southwestern Missouri, thousands of tons of coarse tailings, largely chert, were poured onto huge "chat" piles, many of which remain as a low-priced by-product for some one to put to use. This chat differs mineralogically from the southeastern Missouri chat, which is largely dolomite.

Sphalerite from near Joplin.

Barite ("Tiff")

Barite ("Tiff" in south*east* Missouri, Heavy Spar, Barytes) occurs in Missouri predominantly as a white, quite heavy, soft, non-
metallic mineral which has a high luster on a freshly broken surface.
Slightly bluish "glass" barite or "glass tiff" has been found in smaller
quantity with the more abundant, opaque white material. The
glassy barite may superficially resemble calcite or selenite gypsum,
but in distinction, barite breaks or cleaves to surfaces joining at right
angles and does not effervesce with acid, whereas calcite does effer-

62

vesce in acid and cleaves at oblique angles (rhombohedral cleavage). Gypsum is so soft that it can be scratched very easily with the thumbnail, whereas barite is scratched with difficulty, if at all, by the thumbnail. Notably, again, barite is "heavy," with a specific gravity of about 4.5, whereas calcite, gypsum, limestone, and chert are "lighter," with a specific gravity of about 2.6 to 2.7. Barite has the composition barium sulphate, $BaSO_4$, of which barium oxide constitutes 65.7 per cent.

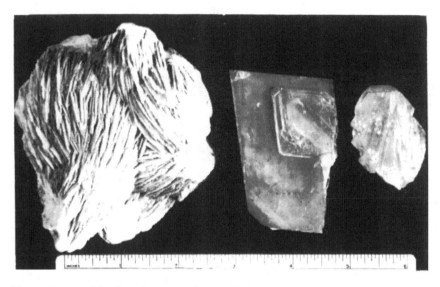

Three pieces of barite, the crested and bladed form at the left, "glass" barite in the center, and a small crystal at the right.

Barite occurs in abundance in the Jefferson-Washington counties district, which furnishes about 80% of Missouri production. Other production comes from near Houston, Texas county, and from the central district—Miller, Moniteau, Morgan, Cole counties, and adjacent territory. In the Jefferson-Washington counties district, it is dug from residual clay over dolomite and is run through washing and concentrating mills which remove the clay and lighter waste rock. Most of the central district production comes from old sinkhole deposits, the ore being also crushed, washed, and concentrated in preparation for shipment. Missouri barite which was produced during 1941 had a value of over $1,300,000 and constituted about 40% of the total United States productions.

Barite is used as a paint pigment and extender, as a flux, as a source of barium in the chemical industry, as a filler in rubber, paper, oil cloth, textiles, and leather, and as a heavy substance in oil well drilling mud. The largest single use is in the manufacture of lithopone paint.

Gypsum

Gypsum is a soft mineral which can be scratched easily with the finger or thumb-nail. It may be glassy or transparent, or may grade into an opaque white body, possibly stained by iron oxide, but it is always very soft. Of the three varieties of gypsum—selenite, alabaster, and satinspar—only the first two have been found in Missouri by the writer. The chemical composition of gypsum is $CaSO_4 \cdot 2H_2O$.

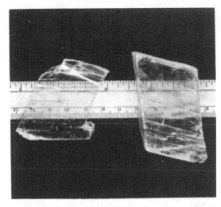

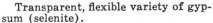

Transparent, flexible variety of gypsum (selenite).

Fine-grained, white, opaque gypsum (alabaster).

The chief use of gypsum is in the manufacture of plaster of paris, during which it is pulverized and heated to drive off part of the water of crystallization so that its composition corresponds to $CaSO_4 \cdot \frac{1}{2}H_2O$. This powder, when mixed with water and poured into a mold, heats and sets; that is, it hardens by taking up enough of the water to restore its original composition.

Although thick, wide-spread beds of gypsum occur in other localities, probably most of the gypsum in Missouri has been secondarily formed, as from the reaction of sulphuric acid from oxidizing pyrite on calcite; and its quantity is limited to small crystals, veins, and crusts in or on other rocks. Gypsum may be an impurity in coal, and some beautiful crystals a few inches long have been found in weathering clay deposits. It therefore cannot be considered as a commercially valuable mineral of this state.

Meteorites

Meteorites, the rock-like specimens which have come to our earth as sparkling meteors in the sky, are perhaps the most prized specimens which the average collector hopes to find, and perhaps more specimens are mistaken for meteorites than for any other geological substance. Meteorites are rare and not easy to find; they are also not easy to determine.

The iron variety is usually a heavy, roughly-pitted, brown, tough, metallic, nickel alloy of iron. Therefore, a positive chemical test for nickel is usually strongly suggestive of a meteoric origin, but confirmation almost requires that a surface be polished and etched with dilute acids to bring out typical and characteristic structures.

The polished and acid-etched surface of an iron meteorite. Shows the Widmänstatten figures characteristic of iron meteorites. (Photo courtesy of American Museum of Natural History, New York).

The stony variety of meteorites usually contains a rock-forming mineral called olivine, beneath its pitted brown surface. In case of either variety, since special equipment is required for final testing and determination, it is recommended that this be done at a laboratory appropriately equipped.

Gold

Gold is not known to occur in Missouri, except for very small quantities which have been carried into the state with the glacial deposits in the north half. Miners have searched carefully, and geologists have studied Missouri rocks intently, comparing them with the gold veins of the western states, but they find no promise of a gold deposit in Missouri. We have been favored with other geological products, but it is a waste of time to search for gold in Missouri.

Silver

Silver has been recovered from ore in the Silver Mines area in Madison county and from the galena of southeastern Missouri. Except for occurrences within the igneous rock area and the lead mining regions, geologists do not expect to find additional silver ore deposits.

Diamonds

No diamond has ever been found in native Missouri rock. It is possible for diamonds to have been carried into the state with the glacial deposits in the northern part, but the probability of finding one, if it did come in, is extremely remote.

Diamonds do occur in one part of Arkansas, but those rocks are strikingly different from all Missouri rocks except in a few localities, having small areas about the size of one's house, in the southeastern part of the state. The writer has received quartz and calcite crystals for testing from persons who hoped they might be diamonds. It is almost a foregone conclusion that diamonds do not occur in Missouri.

A diamond may be recognized by its extreme hardness. It is the hardest substance known, natural or artificial, and will scratch any known substance; but it, in turn, is scratched only by another diamond. Acids do not affect diamonds in the least.

Uranium Minerals

Three uranium-containing minerals, tyuyamunite (pronounced tyew-yuh-moon-ite), possibly carnotite, and metatorbernite, have been found in Missouri but none has been mined commercially. Tyuyamunite and carnotite are canary yellow, powdery minerals so similar in appearance they can be differentiated only by chemical and x-ray properties. Both minerals contain uranium, vanadium, oxygen, water, and one other element, which, if it is calcium, the mineral is tyuyamunite, but if it is potassium the mineral is carnotite. The canary yellow color referred to is distinctly different from the brownish or reddish yellow color of iron oxide minerals. These yellow uranium minerals have been found near Ste. Genevieve along cracks in limestone and in the black shale above the limestone, and in dark, sandy shales near Shelbina, and elsewhere north of the Missouri River.

Black shales (high in organic matter) of marine origin are the most highly radioactive, whereas black shales deposited on land (as with coal), and all shales of other colors are usually lower in radio-activity.

Metatorbernite is a soft, pale apple-green, scaly mineral that has been found in paper-thin cracks in flint fire clay deposits. It contains uranium, copper, phosphorus, oxygen, and water. All of these uranium minerals activate a Geiger counter.

MISCELLANEOUS ROCK STRUCTURES
Concretions

A concretion is an aggregate of inorganic matter in the shape, roughly, of a ball, disc, rod, or irregular nodular body. Usually the aggregation or accumulation started around a small center grain or particle and continued in the growth of layers about it like the shells of an onion, or in the growth of needle-like fibers which radiate from the center like pins stuck into a spherical pin cushion. Concretions vary in size from buck-shot (buck-shot concretions in the soil) to od-dities ten or twenty feet in diameter, or even longer in elongate forms. The variety about one-sixteenth or one-thirty-second of an inch in diameter is called an oolite (pronounced oh-oh-lite). Some chert of southern Missouri, most of the diaspore and burley clay, and a limestone cropping out near Louisiana, Missouri, are made up partly to almost entirely of oolites. See page 29.

Concretions may be composed of pyrite, calcite, limonite, chert, cemented sandstone, or even cemented clay. They are usually recog-nized by their structure after the previously enclosing rock has been eroded. Thus pyrite, limonite, or calcite (limestone) concretions remain after shale has softened and washed away, chert remains after limestone, and strongly cemented "irony" (limonite or hematite) or siliceous sandstone concretions may be found on the outcrop where the softer or less resistant host rock has been carried off. The irregu-lar-shaped, intergrown, nodular limestone concretions (sometimes called "loess-kinder", or loess dolls) in the upper part of loess de-posits along the Missouri and Mississippi Rivers can be found re-maining on rain-washed slopes. Limy, mudstone concretions and brown iron carbonate concretions are abundant in certain localities in northwestern and southeastern Missouri, where they are used as oddities in rock gardens or walls.

Concretions. Dark, limy concretion at left and brassy pyrite at center and right. Note the inter-grown pair in center.

Some concretions are formed at the same general time as the surrounding rock accumulates, but others may be formed years after the surrounding rock has been buried or removed from the environment of its formation. In either case, deposition of the mineral matter follows the pattern of addition or "growth" from inside out. This growth, of course, does not involve a life process like that of a plant or animal. If two or more centers of deposition occur close together, the several growing concretions may touch, intergrow, and develop some weird forms, suggesting organic growth. However odd these curiosities may become, there is no question that they are not fossils, or evidence of life. Probably concretions excite the interest of persons more than any other rock structure.

Ground water, carrying calcium carbonate, silica, or iron compounds in solution, is a great concretion builder. It percolates through sandstone or other permeable rock and slowly leaves behind enveloping layers or additions of mineral matter, until a concretion is formed, to remain hidden from view until its host rock is softened and removed by the action of the weather.

Geodes

A geode is usually a hollow, more or less spherical or ball-shaped shell of mineral and crystal growth which has formed within surrounding rock. Missouri geodes commonly vary in size from hickory nuts to small watermelons, although neither direction of variation is limited. They weather out abundantly at several localities in northeast Missouri from the so-called Warsaw formation, a limy shale. Here they are dark brown, rough and irregular on the outside, but where broken open show many brilliant, glistening faces of intergrown

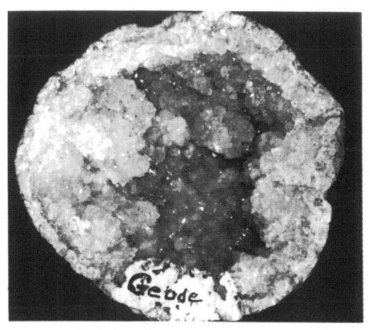

Typical small geode from northeastern Missouri.

quartz crystals. Less frequently calcite, chalcedony, kaolinite, and rarely millerite (nickel sulphide) may occur in Missouri geodes.

The minerals and crystals of a geode grow inward from the walls of a cavity in the rocks. The mineral matter is carried there in solution by ground water and crystallizes out very much more slowly but in the same manner that sugar or salt crystals develop in a saturated solution of those substances. If crystal growth continues until the geode is solid, it may bear superficial resemblance to a concretion, but the latter structure is one which has grown outward. The idea of "growth" in either case is that of mineral crystallization and enlargement, but does not in the least involve life like that of a plant or animal. Geodes have no value or use other than for ornamental purposes.

Fossils

Fossils are also found and collected by persons who are interested in rocks and minerals. The varied remains of plants and animals long since petrified or replaced by mineral matter have stimulated the curiosity and become a source of enjoyment to many persons, from those who merely give a passing glance to the peculiar organic structures in the rocks to those who make a serious hobby or business of collecting and classifying the unreplaceable heritage from the ancient rocks. Fossils are interesting in part because of their variety, for they include petrified wood, shells like those of oysters, fish teeth, foot-prints, amber, dinosaur eggs, coal, imprints of fern leaves, of insects, and of fishes, and the bones of small and gigantic dinosaurs and elephants. In fact, a fossil is any evidence of life in the geologic past preserved in the rocks. Missouri rocks furnish fossils ranging in size from microscopically small fish teeth to the big skeletal remains of the mastodon, an ancestor of the elephant; but the most common ones are the structures and shells of ancient clams, corals, brachiopods, crinoids, and trilobites.

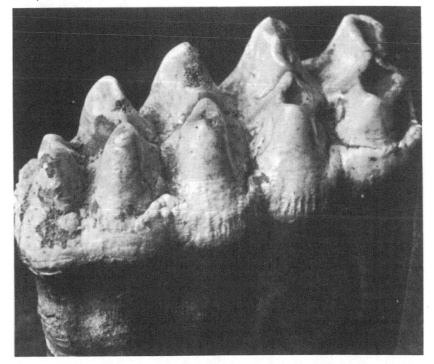

A tooth of a mastodon, about one-half natural size. (Photo courtesy of Mr. J. R. Morrison, Louisiana, Missouri.)

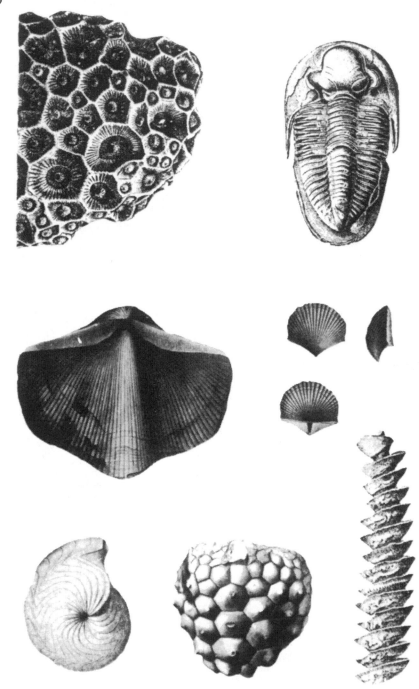

Fossils. Upper row, coral on left, trilobite on right; center row, brachiopods; lower row, coiled cephalapod, crinoid head, and a bryozoan spiral.

The accompanying photographs illustrate a few fossils that may be found within our state, but a thorough, non-technical treatment of Missouri fossils is available in a companion volume to this booklet, "The Common Fossils of Missouri" by Prof. A. G. Unklesbay, Missouri Handbook No. 4.

The study of fossils, or paleontology, is a fascinating branch of geology which extends far beyond the recognition and cataloging of the specimens. It has been found that certain particular fossils occur in rocks of the ages which produce petroleum, and the search for that valuable substance has been directed in many instances by the fossil content of the rocks. Rocks of different ages carry different fossil assemblages, and a man skilled in paleontology utilizes the fossils in dating geologic history like the page numbers in a book of human history. Further, any student of present-day animals and plants is aided in his understanding of them if he knows the fossil record of their ancestors of the long geologic past.

Arrow Heads and Other Indian Artifacts

Arrow heads, scrapers, rock knives and saws which were left by the Indians who formerly lived in Missouri may be found in moderate abundance in many parts of the state. Usually these artifacts are chert in its various colors, white, gray, mottled, reddish, or black (flint). See the discussion of chert on page 34. Chert, because of its conchoidal fracture, lack of cleavage, resistance to chemical weathering, and superior hardness, is an exceptionally useful rock for making tools and weapons.

Hammers and axes of basalt, and arrow heads of rhyolite are less abundant than the chert artifacts.

THE ROCKS OF MISSOURI

Geologists classify rocks into these groups: igneous, sedimentary or metamorphic. Representatives of all three have been described in the preceding pages.

Sedimentary rocks are those whose particles settled down through the air or water to form rocks in layers or beds; hence layered, bedded, or so-called stratified rocks are sedimentary rocks. For instance, the sand and mud settling out of the Gulf of Mexico (or ocean) after being brought in by the Mississippi River is on its way toward becoming sandstone and shale. Limestone is forming off the coast of Florida now. All of these rocks are accumulating in layers. Where one sees regularly-layered or stratified rocks in streams, road cuts, quarries, bluffs or hillsides, he expects them to be sedimentary rocks.

Arrowheads made from white, gray, pink, and black chert. (Courtesy of Mr. A. A. Jeffrey, Columbia, Mo.)

The sedimentary rocks that have been described herein include:

Limestone   Diaspore and Burley clay
Dolomite   Sandstone
Chert   Quartzite
Shale   Travertine
Fire clay   Coal
Flint fire clay

Igneous rocks are those which solidified from a hot liquid which was either forced into older surrounding rocks (intrusive) or discharged on the earth's surface as a lava flow or products from a volcano (extrusive).

The examples given below illustrate the two types. Everyone knows about the extrusive forms from accounts of present-day volcanoes and occasional lava flows, like those of Vesuvius, Parícutin, and Mauna Loa. An intrusion was injected beneath the Yellowstone Park area years ago, and its heat, with steam and gases, is contributing to the unusual natural features which are found in the park and which make it famous.

Igneous rocks in Missouri are:

Granite
Porphyry, Rhyolite, Rhyolite porphyry
Gabbro and Diabase
Basalt

Metamorphic rocks are rocks which have been changed through the effects of tremendous pressure (enough to raise mountains) and high temperature while in the solid state. In most cases a banded rock results. The metamorphic rocks mentioned in this booklet are:

Gneiss
Marble

No doubt it has become apparent to the reader that rocks ordinarily occur in great quantities, that they are composed of multitudes of grains (mineral grains), and that their properties and compositions vary with the different minerals which are present in the grains of the rock. A *rock* can, therefore, be different from a *mineral*. In fact, a rock may be defined as "an aggregate of mineral particles," or more broadly "a typical part of the earth." To focus closer attention on minerals we may discuss them for their own sake below.

MINERALS OF MISSOURI

A mineral is characterized by a constancy of composition and of properties which sets it apart from rocks which vary widely. Minerals may be metallic, like pyrite, or non-metallic, like barite; they may be ore, like galena, or rock-forming, like quartz or feldspar; they may show crystal faces, or they may be fragments with rounded or broken surfaces. A favored definition teaches that "a mineral is a naturally occurring, inorganic substance having a definite chemical composition and definite physical properties, within limits." The Missouri minerals listed herein include:

Quartz	Galena	Pyrite	Orthoclase feldspar
Mica	Barite	Hematite	Microcline feldspar
Calcite	Marcasite	Limonite	Plagioclase feldspar
Dolomite	Carnotite	Gypsum	Metatorbernite
Sphalerite	Tyuyamunite	Pyroxene	

GEOLOGIC VALUES

Although the emphasis in this pamphlet has been on the recognition of Missouri rocks and minerals, it is not out of order to consider the broad values that they contribute to our civilization. Their use as building materials has been noted, but it should be further recognized that as our timber is being rapidly depleted more and more structures will be built out of earth materials. Missouri possesses a wealth of beautiful limestone that is serviceable and readily quarried. Where limestone is not near, there is usually shale or glacial clay which can be used in the manufacture of brick and tile. Permanency will be the keynote of the rock and ceramic structures. Gravel and sand are abundant in Missouri for concrete and other varied uses.

The soil is Missouri's most valuable earth material. Hundreds to thousands of years of normal weathering are required to develop the rocks and minerals and texture of the inorganic fraction of the soil. We should preserve it and prevent disastrous soil erosion.

Aside from these more tangible values, a fascinating and instructive hobby can be made of collecting, arranging, and studying rocks and minerals. One gains a fuller understanding and appreciation of nature from their study. The orderliness, constancy, and interrelation within the rock and mineral "world" is a restful contrast to the one which man often keeps in turmoil. The beauty of a glistening crystal or a polished mineral or stone is as inspiring as a lovely flower, yet it lasts and lasts through centuries, a veritable "rock of ages."

Suggested Collateral Reading Material

Books on Rocks and Minerals

How to Know the Minerals and Rocks, by Pearl; publisher, McGraw-Hill Book Co., New York.

A Field Guide to Rocks and Minerals, by Pough; publisher, Houghton, Mifflin Co., Boston.

Gemstones and Minerals: How and Where To Find Them, by Sinkankas; publisher, Van Nostrand, Princeton, New Jersey.

Look for paper back editions of these and other books which may be widely available.

Fossils

The Common Fossils of Missouri, by A. G. Unklesbay, Missouri Handbook No. 4.

Magazines on Rocks, Minerals, and Fossils

Rocks and Minerals, Box 29, Peekskill, N.Y.

Gems and Minerals, P.O. Box 687, Mentone, Calif.

The Mineralogist, P.O. Box 808, Mentone, Calif.

American Mineralogist, technical official publication of the American Mineralogical Society, Ann Arbor, Michigan, editorial office, Dept. of Mineralogy, University of Michigan.

Books on Mineralogy and Rocks (Technical)

Dana's Manual of Mineralogy, by Hurlbut; publisher, John Wiley & Sons, New York.

Dana's Textbook of Mineralogy, by Ford; publisher, John Wiley & Sons, New York.

Mineralogy, by Berry and Mason; publisher, Freeman & Co., San Francisco.

Rocks and Rock Minerals, by Knopf; publisher John Wiley & Sons, New York.

Guide to the Study of Rocks, by Spock; publisher, Harper & Co., New York.

Books on General Geology

Introduction to Geology, by Branson, Tarr, and Keller; publisher, McGraw-Hill Book Co., New York City. Introduction to College Geology, by Holmes; publisher, Macmillan, New York.

Books on Physical Geology

Geology, by Emmons, Thiel, Stauffer and Allison; publisher McGraw-Hill Book Co., New York.

Principles of Geology, by Gilluly, Woodford, and Waters; publisher, Freeman & Co., San Francisco.

Physical Geology, by Leet and Judson; publisher, Prentice-Hall & Co., New York.

Books on Historical Geology

The Geological Evolution of North America, by Clark and Stearn; publisher, Ronald Press Co., New York.

Time, Life, and Man, by Stirton; publisher, John Wiley & Sons, New York.

These books may be borrowed from public libraries, or purchased from the publishers and retail book stores. At Columbia, the University Book Store, and the Missouri Store Co., sell most of them from shelf stock.

Missouri Geology Publications

Missouri has an excellent State Geological Survey which has published numerous volumes on various geologic topics and areas within the State. Inquiry about these bulletins, circulars, maps, and individually handled correspondence, should be addressed to the:

State Geologist
Missouri Geological Survey
Rolla, Mo.

INDEX